W9-AJP-822

World Book's Animals of the World

Box Turtles
and Other Pond and Marsh Turtles

World Book, Inc.
a Scott Fetzer company
Chicago

Contents

What Is a Pond and Marsh Turtle?

Turtles are reptiles, a kind of cold-blooded animal. The body temperature of a cold-blooded animal stays about the same as the surrounding air and water. Reptiles have a backbone, and they breathe by means of lungs. Most reptiles have skin that is covered with horny plates or scales. Turtles, however, are the only reptile with a shell. This shell protects the turtle from predators (animals that hunt and eat other animals) and is actually part of a turtle's skeleton.

The box turtle forms a genus of turtle (see page 65) called *Terrapene*, which belongs to the pond and marsh turtle family. There are about 90 kinds of pond and marsh turtles in Asia, Europe, North and South America, and northern Africa. Many pond and marsh turtles live in water. Box turtles, however, live on land near ponds and rivers, such as marshes, wetlands, and bogs.

An eastern box turtle

How Does That Shell Work?

Most kinds of turtles can pull their head, legs, and tail into their shell, which serves as a suit of armor. Few other animals with a backbone have such natural protection.

The top shell of a turtle is called the carapace. The bottom shell is called the plastron. The turtle backbone has adapted to allow the neck and tail portions to be very flexible. This allows the turtle to pull its head and tail inside its shell.

The shell covering the back of a box turtle is round. This makes a box turtle look a little like a stocky lizard carrying an upside-down salad bowl on its back. The box turtle's shell is covered in horny plates that fit together in a geometric pattern something like a quilt.

Box turtles are different from many other turtles because they have a hinge on the bottom of their shell. They can pull their legs, head, and tail into their shell and then use this hinge to close up and "box" themselves inside.

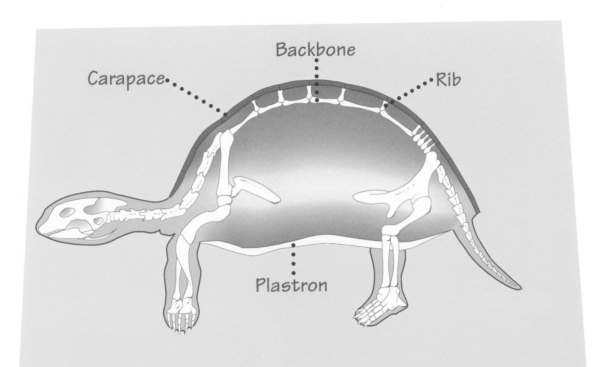

Carapace

Backbone

Rib

Plastron

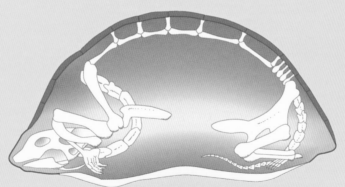

A view of a turtle's bones when
pulled into its shell

Diagram showing how a
turtle pulls into its shell

Where Do Some Types of Box Turtles Live in the Wild?

Box turtles live in the wild in North America and Asia. They live in a variety of habitats where water is readily available. Of the many different kinds of box turtles, four kinds found in the wild in North America are common as pets: the eastern, the three-toed, the Gulf Coast, and the ornate box turtle.

The eastern box turtle, *Terrapene carolina,* lives in the eastern and central United States from Maine south to Georgia and as far west as Illinois, Tennessee, and Alabama. It is also found in Mexico.

The three-toed box turtle, *Terrapene carolina triunguis,* lives in the Mississippi River Valley in several states, including Alabama, Arkansas, Georgia, Kansas, Missouri, and Texas.

The Gulf Coast box turtle, *Terrapene carolina major,* is found in U.S. states along the Gulf of Mexico.

The ornate box turtle, *Terrapene ornata,* lives in the central and south-central United States. You can find it in Illinois, Indiana, and South Dakota into Louisiana and Texas. It is also found in Mexico.

World Map

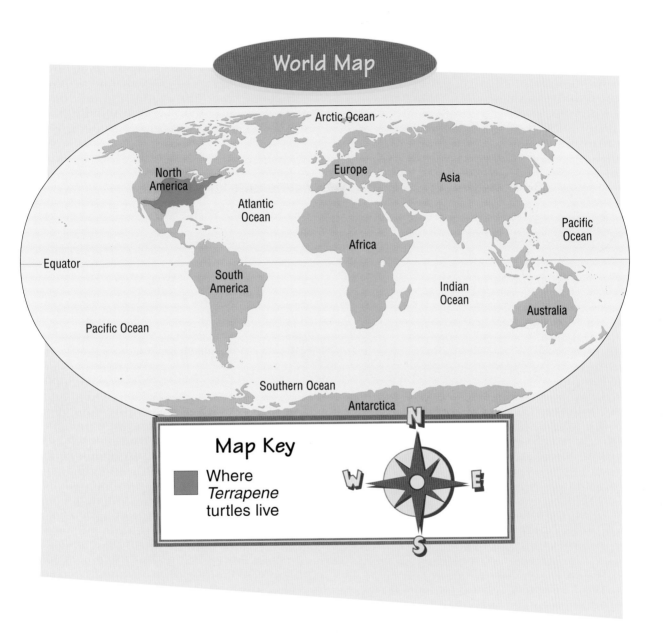

Arctic Ocean

North America

Europe

Asia

Atlantic Ocean

Pacific Ocean

Africa

Equator

South America

Indian Ocean

Australia

Pacific Ocean

Southern Ocean

Antarctica

Map Key

Where *Terrapene* turtles live

N
W E
S

What Kind of Personality Might a Box Turtle Have?

Most box turtles are shy. Some are aggressive. Most enjoy exploring, but some are more active than others.

A pet box turtle will learn quickly who its friends are. A sure way to become such a friend is to be the primary person who feeds the turtle. In time, you can try feeding your turtle treats out of your hand or gently rubbing the back of its head. Some turtles seem to enjoy gentle head massages.

The best way to discover a turtle's true personality, however, is to make sure it has a healthful, safe, clean, and stimulating environment. When healthy and well cared for, a turtle's unique personality will shine right through its shell.

A box turtle
explores the garden

What Should You Look for When Choosing a Box Turtle?

Sadly, many turtles sold in pet stores are in poor health. You can check for signs of illness by looking at a turtle's eyes, shell, skin, and nose. The eyes of a healthy turtle are open, bright, and clear. Its shell is hard and smooth with no deformities (misshapen areas), cracking, or peeling. Its skin is smooth. Its nose and mouth have no liquid coming out.

Gently pick up a turtle. A healthy turtle feels solid and heavy in your hands. If the turtle feels "hollow," it may be malnourished (underfed) or dehydrated (in need of water).

Except during hibernation and breeding season, box turtles usually gorge themselves. Lack of appetite may signal illness. Before buying a turtle, ask the shopkeeper to give it a cricket. The turtle should devour its treat. Some experts also suggest buying a turtle in late spring, summer, or early fall, when you can be sure the turtle is not trying to hibernate.

A healthy eastern box turtle

Can a Box Turtle Found in the Wild Become a Pet?

If you find a box turtle in the wild, do not take it home. A wild box turtle already has a home. Its home is its territory. A turtle knows all the rocks, logs, trees, and ponds in its territory. If you take a turtle from its home, it will suffer from stress and it could die. Additionally, wild turtles can sometimes carry diseases that you can catch.

There are other good reasons to let a wild turtle stay in the wild. Because there is a worrisome decline in wild box turtle populations, many box turtles are protected by law. That means, depending on the area you are in, it could actually be illegal to remove a box turtle from its habitat (the area where an animal lives).

Increasingly, box turtles are being bred in captivity (living under the care of humans) for sale in pet stores. This may help maintain wild populations in the United States and Asia and ensure that turtles in pet stores are healthy and free from bacteria and parasites.

An eastern box turtle
in the wild

What Does a Box Turtle Eat?

A wild box turtle's world is crawling with healthy snacks. Bugs, beetles, worms, slugs, and grubs—all of these are tasty meals to a wild turtle. Wild turtles also eat a lot of berries, other fruits, and vegetation. Because they can forage, or search, for food, wild turtles select a combination of foods.

A pet turtle, like a wild turtle, must have a balanced diet. Making sure your turtle has a proper diet is crucial to its health. You can buy dried food, such as commercial turtle "chow," but it is good to supplement this with fresh foods.

Box turtles need a variety of animal and plant foods. For protein, you can feed your turtle some fish or live, pesticide-free crickets, earthworms, slugs, or bugs. Dark leafy green or brightly colored vegetables are high in minerals and vitamins and should be a central part of your turtle's diet. Collard greens, mustard greens, squashes, sweet potatoes, and carrots are some examples of vegetables that are good for turtles. Some fruits to give include apples, melons, and berries.

A turtle eyes a tasty slug

What Are Some Special Dietary Needs of Box Turtles?

It is hard to know whether a turtle is getting all the nutrients it needs, even when it is fed a balanced diet. Nutrients are the nourishing things in food that supply a living being with the energy it needs. Nutrients also allow the body to build and repair itself. One nutrient a turtle needs is calcium.

Calcium is a building block of bone and shell. A turtle has relatively large calcium requirements since it must maintain both an internal skeleton and an outer shell. A lack of this important mineral results in shell deformities, weak bones, and vulnerability to disease and injury. You should sprinkle a calcium and mineral supplement on your turtle's food regularly. Ask your vet how often your pet will need this supplement.

Another important nutrient is vitamin A. Pet box turtles are prone to vitamin A deficiencies. You can avoid this problem by feeding your turtle plenty of brightly colored green and yellow vegetables.

An eastern box
turtle feeding

How Can You Make Sure Your Turtle Has Enough Water?

Even though box turtles have scales like a lizard, most of them are not desert animals. They need moisture and humidity or they may become very dehydrated. A box turtle must always have access to fresh, clean water for drinking and soaking.

A box turtle needs a large shallow pan of water in its pen. It should be able to get in and out of the pan easily, with the water only going up about one-third of the animal's height. If the water is too deep, the box turtle could drown.

After you bring a new turtle home, you might want to put it in a shallow pan of water for about 15 minutes a day for a week or so. Turtles in pet stores can be dehydrated. By soaking a turtle in ½ inch (1.25 centimeters) of water, it can absorb water and rehydrate itself. If you live in a climate where the air is often dry, you might also want to consider misting your turtle regularly.

Box turtles soaking

23

Where Should a Pet Box Turtle Be Kept?

Keeping your turtle in a small aquarium tank does not make for a very good life for your pet. Ideally, your pet box turtle will live outdoors in a climate similar to the climate in its natural habitat. Your turtle's protective enclosure should contain rocks, hollow logs, and plants similar to its native habitat. There should be places where it can hide and burrow, or dig, and other areas where it can get both sunshine and shade.

A turtle should always have access to fresh, clean water. A turtle also needs to be protected from dogs, raccoons, and other animals that may hurt it.

Depending on where you live, an indoor enclosure may be preferable for your turtle, particularly during late fall, winter, and early spring when it is cold. An indoor pen should have as many features in common with an outdoor pen as possible. The larger its home, the more room your turtle has to explore.

Box turtles in an
outdoor enclosure

How Do You Keep Your Box Turtle's Home Clean and Safe?

Turtles are not unclean animals, but they carry a bacteria called salmonella. This bacteria causes salmonella poisoning, which you can develop if you don't take steps to handle a turtle safely.

It is important to keep your turtle's home spotlessly clean. You should remove a turtle's fecal pellets (waste) from the ground with a scooper every day. It is also very important to change a turtle's water daily. Every week, the enclosure the turtle lives in, and all of the items in this enclosure, should be scrubbed with warm, soapy water. Because of the possible exposure to salmonella, do not clean these items in the kitchen sink! Use a laundry sink, the tub in your bathroom, or an outside hose.

After handling your turtle, you should always wash your hands with soap and water! Be careful not to rub your face or eyes or touch any food when you are cleaning your turtle's home. Wait until after you have washed up.

A turtle's drinking tray (above) is safely cleaned (below)

Why Is Heat Important to a Box Turtle?

Turtles first inhabited Earth during the age of the dinosaurs when the climate was tropical. Because they developed in a warm climate, they still need to be warm. Living in too cold a temperature or being exposed to cold drafts are among the leading causes of death in pet box turtles.

Box turtles are cold-blooded. If a turtle gets too cold, it must move to a warmer spot. If it is too hot, the turtle seeks shade or buries itself in soil.

Your turtle's home should offer it a range of temperatures. If the turtle lives indoors, it needs a heat lamp at one end of its home and a cooler, protected area at the other. In an outdoor home, a turtle needs a place where it can bask in the sun and a shady place that is cooler.

Without warmth, your turtle will lose its appetite and be very sluggish. Proper heat also stimulates a turtle's immune system—the system of cells and tissues that helps a body fight diseases.

A box turtle basks
in the sun

Why Is Ultraviolet Light Important to a Box Turtle?

Sunshine has health benefits beyond simply providing warmth. The sun's rays contain an invisible form of light called ultraviolet. Ultraviolet light is what causes sunburn. However, in turtles as well as people, ultraviolet light also stimulates the production of vitamin D. Without this vitamin, a turtle cannot absorb the calcium from its food.

If your turtle lives indoors, you may want to use a special light bulb that gives off ultraviolet light. You can buy a heat lamp that also produces ultraviolet light. Because heat lamps can dehydrate your turtle, be sure to keep a close eye on your pet for this condition.

tree frogs

A box turtle and tree frogs
under an ultraviolet light

box turtle

How Do Wild Box Turtles Survive Winter?

After all that has been said about the importance of sunlight and heat, you might wonder how wild box turtles survive the winter.

In the wild, turtles hibernate when it is cold. As the days grow shorter in the fall, a box turtle instinctively (without being trained or taught) seeks a safe hiding place, such as its burrow (a hole dug in the ground by an animal for refuge or shelter). The turtle then drifts into a trancelike state in which its heart rate and breathing slow.

Besides helping it to conserve energy, hibernation is part of a turtle's biological rhythm. Hibernation regulates the cues turtles have as to when to breed. In general, turtles that hibernate live longer and are healthier.

Your pet turtle will likely need to hibernate, too. But before you let your turtle hibernate, you should take it to a veterinarian for a checkup and ask for advice on how to help your turtle hibernate.

A box turtle in front
of its burrow

Does a Box Turtle Need Exercise?

Most living creatures benefit from exercise. Turtles are no exception. Your box turtle will be happier and healthier if it has space to crawl about, dig, and hide—activities it would do in nature.

Exercise forces the heart to pump blood, circulating oxygen and nutrients throughout the body. Like people, turtles have muscles that support their joints and allow for movement. These muscles need to be kept active to prevent them from losing their size and strength. Exercise also stimulates a turtle's appetite, ensuring it will eat foods it needs to maintain its bodily functions. And, activity keeps your turtle from becoming fat. Being too fat is bad for a turtle's general health, and it makes a turtle less able to completely pull its head and legs into its shell.

Don't think your turtle will jog around the yard, however. Turtles are slow-moving creatures. Some gentle walking and climbing will be enough exertion for a turtle.

A box turtle climbing

How Can You Tell If Your Turtle Is Male or Female?

Male and female turtles look basically the same. But if you know what to look for, you can tell if your turtle is a "she" or a "he."

Female box turtles often have yellowish-brown eyes. Their tails are shorter than those of male box turtles. The hind claws of female turtles are slender and straighter.

Males often have red eyes. Their tails tend to be thicker and longer. Their hind claws are sometimes curved like an eagle's talons.

In many box turtles, females have a flat spot on the bottom of their shell. This part of the shell on males is slightly concave, or indented.

A male (right) and female (left) box turtle

What Should You Do If Your Box Turtle Lays Eggs?

If your box turtle lays eggs, it is best to remove them from the mother's home and incubate the eggs under a special heating lamp. The eggs will hatch in about 70 to 85 days. Newborn hatchlings will be about 1½ inches (4 centimeters) long when they emerge.

When ready to hatch, a young turtle cracks its shell using its legs and a sharp point under its nostrils, called an egg tooth. The egg tooth is not actually a tooth, and it falls off soon after the turtle hatches.

After tearing a hole in its shell, a turtle may stay in its egg for a few hours or even a couple of days. After it hatches, the turtle will have a strange sac attached to its belly. Do not remove it. It is a yolk sac, a "storage tank" of nutrition for the hatchling.

An ornate box turtle hatching

How Do You Care for Box Turtle Hatchlings?

Motherhood is over pretty quickly for a female box turtle. She lays her eggs, covers them in soil, and walks off. Neither she nor the father turtle interact with their young, at least as far as biologists (scientists who study living things) know.

Turtles are born knowing everything they need to know to make it on their own. They can walk and forage for food. They don't need a mother, or you, to teach them these things.

Because newborn turtles are fragile, however, it is a good idea to move them to a separate tank for some days. You want to make sure hatchlings are warm, protected from drafts, well fed, given plenty of water, and protected from predators.

An eastern box turtle laying an egg in a nest

What Is the Difference Between Turtles and Tortoises?

Tortoises are turtles that are strictly land animals. They take drinks and short baths at watering holes, but their behavior shows a strong preference for walking about on land. They never dip their head underwater or bathe for long periods.

Tortoises also tend to be bigger than turtles and live longer. Their shells are more domed than turtles and their hind legs are shaped like those of an elephant. Many tortoises also have horny scales on their front legs.

The Galapagos tortoise that lives on islands off Ecuador in South America is perhaps the most famous tortoise. It can weigh more than 500 pounds (227 kilograms) and live to be 150 years old. "Galapagos" means tortoise in Spanish.

Galapagos tortoises

How Can You Tell What Kind of Box Turtle You Have?

If you have a pet box turtle, it is likely either an eastern, ornate, three-toed, or Gulf Coast box turtle.

If your turtle has a lot of colorful lines, dots, and splotches on its shell, it may be an eastern box turtle. If its colorful markings consist of yellow lines radiating out from the plates on its shell, it may be an ornate box turtle. Some other types of box turtles also have yellow radiating lines, though, so this is not a sure way to identify an ornate box turtle.

A three-toed box turtle can sometimes be easy to identify. It often has three toes on its hind legs. Some other box turtles have three toes, though, so this is not a sure sign that it is a three-toed turtle. And, to add more confusion, some three-toed turtles have four toes.

If none of these descriptions fit, you may have a Gulf Coast box turtle. These turtles usually have no pattern on their shell and are the largest of the four species (kinds) of box turtle.

An eastern box turtle

An ornate box turtle

A three-toed box turtle

A Gulf Coast box turtle

Different types of
box turtles

What Is a Pond Slider?

There are other types of pond and marsh turtles besides box turtles—one is the pond slider. Pond sliders are "basking turtles" that live near permanent bodies of water, such as ponds and rivers. These turtles are very fond of gathering in groups on logs and rocks and basking—that is, warming themselves—in the sun. Pond sliders are also good swimmers.

Pond sliders are found in the southern and central United States. There is also a Big Bend slider that lives along the upper Rio Grande around the border of the United States and Mexico. Other kinds of sliders can be found in Mexico, Central America, South America, and on islands in the Caribbean Sea.

One type of pond slider that is fairly easy to recognize is the red-eared slider. These turtles often have bright red streaks behind their eyes. Sadly, at one time people treated red-eared sliders somewhat as "disposable" pets. There is now greater awareness of how to take proper care of these and other kinds of turtles.

A red-eared slider

What Is a Chicken Turtle?

Another member of the pond and marsh turtle family is the chicken turtle. A chicken turtle is a small, aquatic turtle that feeds on plants, tadpoles, and crayfish. It is found along waterways in the southeastern and central United States.

It is called a chicken turtle because some say its flesh is mild and tasty, like chicken.

A chicken turtle has a very long neck. When this turtle stretches its neck, it looks like a snake slithering out from a shell. A chicken turtle also has "striped pants." Its legs and rump have yellow stripes on them.

Chicken turtles are rare in some places and so are protected in the wild. You should not, therefore, buy a chicken turtle. In addition, some chicken turtles tend to bite. Others are shy around people, so this species does not make an ideal pet.

A chicken turtle

What Is a Map Turtle?

A map turtle is also a pond and marsh turtle. This aquatic turtle basks on fallen trees and deadwood in lakes and rivers in the central and southeastern United States and in Quebec in Canada. The map turtle rarely leaves its water home for land. It is also a shy turtle. A basking map turtle will quickly vanish beneath the water's surface if startled by people.

Map turtles get their name from the intricate line patterns on their shell, which look like markings on a map. Some map turtles also have spinelike projections along the back of their shell. These turtles, called sawbacks, look something like a tiny dinosaur.

Map turtles are more sensitive to water quality than other aquatic turtles.

A map turtle

Why Is There a Turtle Crisis in Asia?

Asia has an astounding variety of pond and marsh turtles. The Chinese box turtle and the Malayan box turtle are two examples of Asian turtles that are kept as pets.

Rapid economic growth and land development in many parts of Asia have reduced the turtle's wild habitat. Additionally, many turtles throughout Asia are captured for food, for use in medicines, and for export for the pet trade. For example, the Malayan box turtles shown at right were part of a cargo of some 10,000 turtles that were being shipped illegally for the pet trade. The shipment was intercepted by customs agents.

With the loss of habitat and so many turtles being captured, many species of Asian turtles are in peril. An international treaty that was created to regulate trade in threatened plant life and wildlife restricts the export of box turtles. These restrictions apply both to box turtles that are native to Asia and to those native to the United States. Many countries have signed this treaty and are working to protect box turtles.

Malayan box turtles

For How Long Can Box Turtles Live?

Turtles are famous for aging gracefully. In fact, their lifespan is so impressively long that scientists study turtles to gain insights into the aging process in people.

If given proper care, a box turtle can easily live 30 or 40 years. Some have lived to be more than 100. You might have a very long friendship with your turtle. In fact, your turtle could live to see you retire.

While your turtle could outlive you, it won't keep growing bigger through the years. When they are fully grown, most kinds of pet box turtles are between 4 to 8 inches (10 to 20 centimeters) long. And, most box turtles are fully grown by the time they are around 5 or 6 years old.

A box turtle

What Are Some Common Signs of Illness in Turtles?

Any change in your turtle's behavior or appetite should cause you to watch it closely. It may be a sign of illness. Here are some things to examine:

- Listen to your turtle breathe. If a turtle is wheezing, rasping, breathing with its mouth open, or if there is liquid around its nostrils, the turtle may have a respiratory infection.

- Look at your turtle's shell and skin. Any shell deformities, softening of the shell, or peeling of the skin could indicate a nutritional problem.

- Also look in your turtle's eyes. Swollen or cloudy eyes may indicate an infection or a deficiency of vitamin A.

- Check your turtle's solid waste. It should be solid and well formed. If not, take samples to your vet for tests. Parasites can cause diarrhea.

- When in doubt, take your turtle to a vet. Often, sick turtles do not show symptoms until they are seriously ill.

Examining a box turtle

What Routine Veterinary Care Is Needed?

Even if they don't show it, many turtles sold as pets are sick, underweight, and undernourished. You should take your turtle to a veterinarian who is knowledgeable about turtles soon after you buy it.

Turtles can carry worms and other parasites. You should take a fecal sample (a sample of solid waste) to the vet, who will test the sample for these problems. The vet can give your turtle medicine that will rid it of most kinds of parasites.

While you are there, your vet will also examine your turtle's shell and skin for evidence of nutritional deficiencies, injury, or infection. Your turtle's mouth may also be opened for signs of mouth rot—a swelling and redness of the mouth that happens in reptiles. If your turtle is dehydrated or underweight, your vet will let you know.

Ask your veterinarian how often you should bring your turtle in for checkups. Also, ask your vet what measures to take to keep your specific type of turtle healthy and happy.

A vet examining a box turtle

What Are Your Responsibilities as an Owner?

Your turtle is not a toy. It is a living creature that knows when it is thirsty, hungry, and sleepy. It feels pain and will try to protect itself from danger. If you ignore your turtle, its life will be short, and it will suffer.

As an owner, it is your responsibility to give your turtle the best home and life you can. You must feed it nutritious foods, keep its living quarters clean, and provide it with enough space. You must take it to the veterinarian regularly and protect it from animals that might hurt it. If you go on vacation, you must make appropriate arrangements.

Your turtle will fare better if you educate yourself about its natural history, biology, and captive care. Also, ask yourself, "What can I do to make my turtle a little happier?" Maybe get it a few raspberries? Show it you care by keeping its home tidy? If you do such things as these, it is likely that you and your box turtle will have a very long friendship.

An eastern box turtle

Turtle Fun Facts

→ Though hard, a turtle's shell is sensitive when touched.

→ Turtles do not have teeth. Their mouth is technically a beak.

→ If you are allergic to cats or dogs, a turtle may make a good pet. Turtles do not trigger allergies in humans.

→ All turtles, even sea turtles, lay their eggs on land.

→ Many ancient people believed they could foresee the future by reading turtle shells.

→ The gender of a box turtle is not determined by its genes. The temperature at which an egg is incubated is what determines a box turtle's gender.

→ A group of turtles is called a "bale."

Glossary

aquatic Growing or living in water.

breeding season The time of year when male and female animals mate.

captivity In animals, living under the care of humans and not in the wild.

dehydrated In living things, to be in need of water.

forage To hunt or search for food.

habitat The area where an animal lives, which contains everything the animal needs to survive.

hatchling A very young turtle only recently hatched from its shell.

hibernation When an animal spends a period or a season in a state of deep sleep; often, the animal's metabolism and body temperature are lowered when hibernating.

incubate To keep eggs warm so that they will hatch.

parasite An organism (living creature) that feeds on and lives on or in the body of another organism, often causing harm to the being on which it feeds.

pesticide A chemical that is used to kill insects.

reptile Any one of a class of cold-blooded animals with a backbone that breathes by means of lungs and usually has skin covered with horny plates or scales. Alligators, crocodiles, lizards, snakes, and turtles are reptiles.

species A group of animals that have certain permanent characteristics in common and that are able to produce offspring.

tropical An animal or plant that lives in (or comes from) regions near Earth's equator. These regions have mostly warm temperatures the year around and plentiful rainfall.

(**Boldface** indicates a photo, map, or illustration.)

Index

For more information about Box Turtles and Other Pond and Marsh Turtles, try these resources:

Box Turtles: Facts & Advice on Care and Breeding (Reptile and Amphibian Keeper's Guide), by Richard and Patricia Bartlett, Barron's Educational Series, 2001

Box Turtles: Keeping and Breeding Them in Captivity by Jordan Patterson, Chelsea House Publications, 1998

Tortoises and Box Turtles: A Complete Pet Owner's Manual, by Hartmut Wilke, Barron's Educational Series, 2000

http://animaldiversity.ummz.umich.edu/site/accounts/information/Terrapene_carolina.html

http://nationalzoo.si.edu/Animals/ReptilesAmphibians/Facts/FactSheets/Easternboxturtle.cfm

http://www.chelonia.org/articles/Terrapenecare.htm

Turtle Classification

Scientists classify animals by placing them into groups. The animal kingdom is a group that contains all the world's animals. Phylum, class, order, and family are smaller groups. Each phylum contains many classes. A class contains orders, an order contains families, and a family contains genuses. One or more species belong to each genus. Each species has its own scientific name. (The abbreviation "spp." after a genus name indicates that a group of species from a genus is being discussed.) Here is how the animals in this book fit into this system.

Animals with backbones and their relatives (Phylum Chordata)
Reptiles (Class Reptilia)
Turtles and their relatives (Order Testudines)

Pond and marsh turtles and their relatives (Family Emydidae)

New World pond and marsh turtles (Subfamily Emydinae)

Eastern box turtle	*Terrapene carolina*
Gulf Coast box turtle	*Terrapene carolina major*
Three-toed box turtle	*Terrapene carolina triunguis*
Ornate box turtle	*Terrapene ornata*

Chicken turtle	*Deirochelys reticularia*
Map turtles	*Graptemys* spp.
Big Bend slider	*Trachemys gaigeae*
Red-eared slider	*Trachemys scripta elegans*

Eurasian pond and river turtles (Subfamily Batagurinae)

Malayan box turtle	*Cuora amboinensis*
Chinese box turtle	*Cuora trifasciata*

Tortoises (Family Testudinidae)

Galapagos tortoise	*Geochelone nigra*